Elie Wiesel

Elie Wiesel

Caroline Lazo

Peacemakers

DILLON PRESS
New York

Maxwell Macmillan Canada
Toronto

Maxwell Macmillan International
New York Oxford Singapore Sydney

To Norman

The author and publisher would like to give special thanks to Elie Wiesel for his help with this project.

Photo Credits

AP—Wide World Photos: Cover, 8, 14, 48, 53
The Bettmann Archive: 2, 6, 11, 13, 20, 23, 26, 29, 33, 41, 45, 51, 56-57, 60
Rijksinstituut voor Oorlogsdocumentatie, Amsterdam: 36, 39

Book design by Carol Matsuyama

Library of Congress Cataloging-in-Publication Data

Lazo, Caroline Evensen.
    Elie Wiesel / by Caroline Lazo. — 1st ed.
      p. cm.
    Includes bibliographical references and index.
    ISBN 0-87518-636-X   0-382-24715-9 (pbk.)
    1. Wiesel, Elie, 1928-   —Biography—Juvenile literature. 2. Authors, French—20th century—Biography—Juvenile literature. 3. Holocaust sur- vivors—Biography—Juvenile literature. 4. Jewish authors—Biography— Juvenile literature. [1. Wiesel, Elie, 1928-   2. Authors, French. 3. Holocaust, Jewish (1939-1945)] I. Title.
PQ2683.I32Z73   1994
813'.54—dc20
[B]   93-44473

Summary: A biography of author and educator Elie Wiesel, who won the Nobel Peace Prize in 1986 for his writings and work on behalf of victims and survivors of the Holocaust.

Dillon Press   Maxwell Macmillan Canada, Inc.
Macmillan Publishing Company 1200 Eglinton Avenue East
866 Third Avenue   Suite 200
New York, NY 10022   Don Mills, Ontario M3C 3N1

Macmillan Publishing Company is part of the Maxwell Communication Group of Companies.

First Edition

Printed in the United States of America

10 9 8 7 6 5 4 3 2 1

Evil is not passive, but active. It is self-assertive, and it strives to conquer. If it is not halted ... it can triumph, just as desert can triumph over fertile land, or the sea over a sandy beach.

—Elie Wiesel

Elie and Marion Wiesel are greeted by the mayor of Paris as Elie accepts one of the many awards he has received for his work.

Contents

Introduction

The little town of Sighet is almost impossible to find on a map of Rumania. But we know it is there, because in countless books and stories—evoking both heartache and hope—Elie Wiesel has told us so.

Sighet, located in Europe's Carpathian Mountains, has special meaning for Elie Wiesel—not because of happy childhood memories but because of the horror that destroyed them. That horror was the Holocaust, Adolf Hitler's systematic extermination of Jews and other innocent people in Nazi-occupied territories before and during World War II. Six million Jews died in the Holocaust, and Elie Wiesel's parents and sister were among them. Since then he has become the victims' most eloquent spokesman, committed to doing what he can to end the hatred, prejudice, and indifference that spawned the most evil event of the 20th century.

It was Wiesel who named the tragedy the Holocaust. And because he survived it, he wants to "give testimony, to bear witness" so that such an evil event will never happen again. His efforts to end oppression in the world have earned him international

Elie Wiesel testifies at a hearing investigating war crimes committed during the Gulf War.

acclaim—including the Nobel Peace Prize. The prize, he believes, helps to illuminate his work and to remind us that unless we pay attention to peace and have the "courage to care" about the human rights of others, men like Hitler could rise again.

By spring 1944, Hitler had ordered all Jews in Sighet (and other towns throughout Europe) to concentration camps. The camps, they were told, were places of safety during the war in Europe. But in fact they were death camps—where Hitler carried out his evil plan to "purify" the world by killing all those who didn't fit the mold of his Aryan (Nordic or Gentile) "master race." To convince the Christian population of the rightness of his plan, Hitler cleverly adopted the work camp idea used in the 1500s by German Protestant reformer Martin Luther. (At that time, Jews who refused to convert to Luther's Protestant faith were sent to work camps, where most of them starved to death.)

Auschwitz, the most well-known death camp, became a symbol for all of Hitler's killing fields. But how could such places exist without being detected?

President Ronald Reagan presents Elie Wiesel with a Congressional Gold Medal for his work.

Or were they known and purposely ignored? If so, why? Though outsiders had no access to the camps, soldiers and pilots during World War II knew about them. American and European leaders knew about them. Pope Pius XII knew about them. The surrounding

Christian communities could not escape the smell of death in the air. They knew about them. So how could the camps continue? "Auschwitz remains a question without an answer," Elie Wiesel says. "All we can do is ask questions and wonder." And never forget. "To forget," he wrote, "means a victory for the enemy."

As professor of the humanities at Boston University, and founding chairman of the Holocaust Memorial Council, Wiesel encourages people to ask questions and to learn as much as possible about the past so that their world will be a safer place in the future. "Wherever there is oppression," he says, "that place must become the center of the universe." And he insists, "If the voices of the victims are stifled, we must lend them ours."

"Great writer though he is," theologian Robert McAfee Brown wrote, "Wiesel is also a peacemaker, one whose words . . . attain the quality of deeds." Today Wiesel combines his words and actions to bring peace to suffering people around the world. He has traveled to South Africa, India, Cambodia, and Bosnia—"wherever there is oppression"—to help

Elie Wiesel discusses the human rights situation in Bosnia with that country's president, Alija Izetbegovic.

restore human rights and hope. When asked why he works so hard for others, not just Jews, he replied simply, "Because I have seen what I have seen is why I do what I do." And he reminds us: "When all hope is gone, Jews invent new hopes. Even in the midst of despair, we attempt to justify hope."

Or in the words of Albert Camus, one of Wiesel's favorite writers: "In the depths of winter, I learned that within me there lay an invincible summer."

Supreme Court Justice Sandra Day O'Connor swears in Elie Wiesel as chairman of the United States Holocaust Memorial Council.

14

From Hatred to Hope

Even in ancient Rome, before the birth of Christ, Jews suffered from anti-Semitism (hostility toward people of the eastern Mediterranean area). The Jews' belief in one God conflicted with the existing pagan (nonreligious) philosophy of the Romans. "The Romans," Elie Wiesel reminds us, "were pagans . . . not Christians, yet they hated the Jews. It cannot be said, therefore, that Christianity alone spawned the hatred of the Jews that we see throughout history . . . although Christianity certainly contributed to broadening it."

Jews were Christ's first followers, but when Christ was killed, Saint Paul blamed the Jews, and in doing so freed the Romans from any responsibility or guilt. The New Testament of the Bible clearly answers the question of right and wrong. Christians were right; Jews were wrong. And that interpretation of the facts fostered anti-Semitism. (Not until 1965 did the Church officially remove from the Jews any blame for Christ's death.)

Like an endless dark shadow, anti-Semitism followed Christianity as it spread throughout Europe. In 1095, under the rule of Pope Urban II, crusaders burned down synagogues as Jews prayed inside. No one survived. In England during the reign of Richard the Lionhearted (1189–1199), Jews were murdered if they refused to join the crusaders. In 1478 thousands more were tortured in the notorious Spanish Inquisition—the institution known for its cruel punishment of those who opposed the pope. In Germany, Jewish literature was burned, and posters depicting Jews as devils with horns were pasted on building walls.

Though the Jews were being murdered by the Christians, they themselves were being portrayed as murderers! Such myths about the Jews—that they were evil—spread quickly through Christian communities and passed on from generation to generation. And as the dark shadow widened, Jews became more isolated. They were not allowed to own land, but they could own shops or become money lenders. Yet when they became experts in those jobs, Christians ridiculed and stereotyped them. ("Even when we win, we lose!" Elie Wiesel once said.) Martin Luther gave the Jews a chance to get out of the ghettos (restricted living areas) only if they converted to the new Protestant faith. Almost all refused. Persecution continued, and by the end of the Middle Ages, Jews were hated throughout Europe. But defeated? No.

By the 19th century, Jews, though a minority, had become a major part of European life. Their remarkable achievements in the sciences, literature, banking, and music stunned the world. Giants like Einstein, Freud, and Mahler changed the image of the Jew—from a symbol of evil to a subject of envy. They had become experts in a variety of fields, and their contributions to society—from medicine to movie making—continued to make history in the 20th century.

But hatred based on thousand-year-old myths and superstitions did not go away. Anti-Semitism became less obvious, but it was still there. It could be heard, for example, in the works of German composer-writer Richard Wagner—who was admired by Adolf Hitler. And it was Hitler who revived, and went far beyond, the past persecution of the Jews. Though Hitler's crusade was racial (to develop his "master race") rather than religious, the fact remains: His

Eastern Europe at the time of World War II

killers were mostly Christians, and his victims were mostly Jews.

Like Hitler, Joseph Stalin, who became Soviet leader in the late 1920s, was fanatic about the Jews, and reportedly had planned to send them all to Siberia, where they would have starved. But his death in 1953 saved them from that fate. Still, discrimination and human rights violations continued in Russia; Jews continued to suffer there. Hadn't they suffered enough? Hadn't six million Jews been murdered during Hitler's evil reign? How could such hatred continue?

With democracy on the march now and human rights committees at work around the world, why does anti-Semitism still exist? Perhaps, Elie Wiesel suggests, Jews will always be a reminder of the Holocaust, of the awful silence of the bystanders—and the guilt that many still feel but can't bear to face.

But Wiesel doesn't believe in collective guilt. He does not believe that people today—especially the German youth—should feel guilty for crimes committed before they were even born. Around the world, Elie Wiesel encourages reconciliation. And as a

"messenger to all humanity," Robert McAfee Brown writes, Wiesel carries a message of solidarity and hope: "He gives us a moral vision with which we can begin to re-create a new future out of the debris of history."

Of the six million Jews killed by Hitler's Nazi officers, one million were children. Elie Wiesel was just a teenager when he was sent to Auschwitz— only 15 years old when he lost his mother, father, little sister, and almost everyone he knew in Sighet. "I am convinced," he wrote, "that one day the dead themselves will speak. . . . Perhaps they will speak through us. But one day they will speak, and on that day the earth will tremble."

He also wrote:

> The day will come—I hope soon—when we shall all understand that suffering can elevate man as well as diminish him. . . . In the final analysis, it is not given to us to bring suffering to an end—that frequently is beyond us—but we can humanize it. To turn it into dialogue rather than sword depends only on us, on you.

Elie Wiesel throws out the first ball at the second game of the 1986 World Series.

Will we succeed? I yearn for this with all my heart. . . . Help us not to despair of you. Or of mankind. And then perhaps, out of our reconciliation, a great hope will be born.

Dodye Feig's Grandson

Eliezer (Elie) Wiesel was born on September 30, 1928, in the little town of Sighet "in the shadow of the Carpathian Mountains." Fifteen thousand Jews—bonded by joys and sorrows, past and present—lived in that quiet town in Transylvania, now a part of Rumania. Following Jewish tradition, their lives revolved around their families and care of the children—the parents' most important concern.

Though he was "almost pathologically shy" as a child, young Elie showed promise as a writer. At the

Even as a child, Elie Wiesel was concerned with the issues that would later become his life's work and earn him a Nobel Peace Prize.

age of 12 he wrote a book about his views of the Bible. And when he wasn't writing, he was reading or listening to stories told by his relatives—especially by his grandfather, Dovid Feig, affectionately called Dodye. Elie would always want to write, but he never dreamed that someday his writing would have to reveal such terror and sadness—or that he would ever become world-famous because of it. Yet even as a young boy Elie's large, dark eyes looked unusually sad—as if, some believe, he foresaw tragedy and was destined to survive to tell about it. But he disagrees with such "destination" theories. His survival, he said, was due to "pure chance."

Elie's parents, Shlomo and Sarah (Feig) Wiesel, were shopkeepers in Sighet, and after school his older sisters, Hilda and Batya, assisted them. But Elie was encouraged to write, study the Talmud and the Torah, and to pursue his love of learning. And it was his grandfather, Dodye Feig, whose storytelling captivated him and became the chief inspiration behind his later work.

"In the Hasidic kingdom of Wizsnitz he was a

celebrity, and in that circle I am still today identified as 'Dodye Feig's grandson,'" Wiesel wrote in *A Jew Today.* "People loved him. Especially for his songs; he knew more songs than all the cantors at the Rebbe's court. . . . People also loved him for his kindness. He gave freely of himself. No one ever left him empty-handed. . . . He would say, 'The poorest among the faithful finds something to share.'" Above all, he wrote, "Dodye Feig was loved because of his passion for life, for people, trees, books. He illuminated souls by his mere presence." And he captured the heart of his grandson forever.

Dodye Feig was a "robust man, full of verve" and "with a beard as white as snow." But because he lived in another town, Elie was unable to visit him as often as he wanted. His trips with his mother to Dodye's farm were unforgettable, but once, he recalls vividly, he couldn't wait for his mother to take him there, so he ran away from home to see him. "Without humiliating me or scolding me, he questioned me about the reasons for my escapade. I answered as best I could: 'I missed you, Grandfather.'—'Is that the real reason, the

Former president Jimmy Carter joins Elie Wiesel for a memorial remembering the millions of people killed in concentration camps during World War II.

only one?'—'Yes, Grandfather, the only one.'—'Are you sure it wasn't out of spite? Did someone insult you at school? Were you scolded at home? Could you have quarreled with your father?'—'No, grandfather. I wanted to see you, that's all.'—'All right then, I'm glad. I used to run away sometimes too. . . .' And he would tell me of his childhood, making me proud to be judged worthy of his confidences. I felt I had run away from home solely to come and collect his words."

One special night during Dodye's visit to Sighet to celebrate the Shabbat (holy day), he and Elie's father discussed the rising tide of anti-Semitism in Europe. Fascists had seized control of Budapest, Hungary—Rumania's next-door neighbor. And anti-Jewish slogans and statements appeared everywhere, designed to brainwash the people, to prepare them for Hitler's "purification" scheme, which meant the killing of the Jews. "Every day," Elie Wiesel wrote, "the sky got darker. 'And God?' asked my father. 'And man?' answered my grandfather. . . . 'God is God and His ways are sometimes incomprehensible—and so they must be. If you could always understand what He is doing, He would not be what He is, you would not be what you are.'"

"[That] was our last Shabbat together," Elie wrote. He never saw his grandfather again.

Hitler's killers had begun to sweep through

Europe. If you were Jewish—man, woman, or child—you were labeled with a yellow star and, though no one dared to believe it, programmed for torture and death. By killing the Jews and other "misfits," Hitler would realize his dream of an all-Aryan world . . . or so he thought. And Elie Wiesel would never forget that last Shabbat and the questions asked by his father and grandfather:

"Where is God?"

"Where is man?"

To the Railway Station

When Hitler took control of Germany in 1933, many Jews feared his power and fled the country. More than 30,000 left during the first year of his dictator-

Wearing a United Nations helmet and protective vest, Elie Wiesel inspects conditions in the war-torn city of Sarajevo.

ship. Yet many more stayed behind; they believed that his anti-Semitic regime couldn't last long, and they wanted to hold on to their homeland as long as possible. Besides, anti-Semitism was nothing new to the

Jews in Europe; they had endured it for centuries. But death camps? Burning people alive? Tossing beaten children into open graves, on top of corpses—some, still breathing? Who but a madman would assert that such evil acts were taking place in civilized Europe? Elie Wiesel knew such a man.

People called him Moshe the Beadle. He did maintenance work in a synagogue in Sighet. Like Elie's grandfather, Moshe had stories to tell and words of wisdom that endeared him to the whole community. And his kindness, knowledge, and faith in God enchanted 12-year-old Elie Wiesel. In his book *Night,* Professor Wiesel recalls this special friend, "with his waiflike timidity [who] made people smile":

> He explained to me with great insistence that every question possessed a power that did not lie in the answer. "Man raises himself toward God by the questions he asks of Him," he was fond of repeating. "That is the true dialogue. Man questions God and God answers. But we don't understand His answers. We can't under-

stand them, because they come from the depths of the soul. . . . You will find the true answers, Eliezer, only within yourself!" And why do you pray, Moshe? I asked him. "I pray to the God within me that he will give me the strength to ask the right questions."

Moshe the Beadle became both friend and instructor to young Elie. It was he who introduced him to the Zohar, the cabalistic books—a study that philosopher Maimonides said could start only at the age of 30. Elie loved and respected Moshe for ignoring his young age and for responding to his passion for learning. But Moshe was a foreigner in Sighet, and Hitler's extermination of Jews began with the deportation of all foreigners from the towns he conquered. So one day Moshe simply vanished, as all deportees seemed to do—quietly in the night.

Months later Elie saw Moshe back in Sighet—sitting outside the synagogue where he once worked. He told Elie what had happened to him after he was deported:

31

The train full of deportees had crossed the Hungarian frontier, and on Polish territory had been taken in charge by the gestapo. There it had stopped. The Jews had to get out and climb into lorries. The lorries drove toward a forest. The Jews were made to get out. They were made to dig huge graves. And when they had finished . . . the gestapo slaughtered their prisoners. Each one had to go up to the hole and present his neck. Babies were thrown into the air and machine gunners used them as targets. This was in the forest of Galicia, near Kolomaye.

When Moshe was shot in the leg, he fell in the pit, pretending to be dead. When he didn't move, the gestapo left him there. When they finished their deadly game, they moved on. And Moshe crawled out of the grave and escaped through the forest. "Through long days and nights," Elie wrote, "Moshe went from one Jewish house to another, telling the story of Malka, the young girl who had taken three days to die, and of

General Colin Powell, then head of the U.S. Joint Chiefs of Staff, speaks with Elie Wiesel before ceremonies at Yeshiva University.

Tobias, the tailor, who had begged to be killed before his sons."

But no one believed Moshe's bizarre tales. They thought he had lost his mind. And in Sighet he was no longer known as Moshe the Beadle. From then on he was called Moshe the Madman, pitied and ignored. But

Moshe kept on talking, kept on warning. When the Hungarian police stormed into Sighet and confiscated all valuables—jewelry, gold, in particular—from the Jews, Moshe told Elie's father, "I warned you!" Still, no one saw the police action as a step toward total evacuation and death. Poor Moshe, they said; he had gone mad.

It was part of Hitler's strategy to kill people secretly and in stages. Mass murders would attract attention, world attention. He couldn't risk retaliation from the Allies (the United States, Great Britain, France, and Russia). Though, eventually, he conducted mass killings daily, the camps were remotely located, and the Allies focused on destroying Hitler's military power rather than saving the lives of the Jews. And most people didn't believe the "rumors" that the camps even existed. At the same time, many residents in nearby towns recognized the smell of death that filled the air as Hitler switched from shooting the Jews to gassing them in ovens. (The latter method was more impersonal and easier on the Nazi officers, he claimed.) Wiesel tells us that the Christian officers would go to church between killings—to be forgiven! That way, they could continue to kill with a clear conscience. Without any retaliation from the Allies, they were completely free to do so. And they did.

In 1944 ghettos were established in Sighet . . . the second stage of Hitler's program. Fenced in by barbed wire, the Jews drew closer together both physically and spiritually. They carried on their lives—always hoping and expecting things to get better. Surely Hitler would be defeated once Russia entered the war, they believed. And they kept on hoping and believing.

Elie continued to read, write, and study. And like most of the Jewish community, his family believed that Nazis wouldn't bother with a small, distant town like Sighet. Though they had to wear yellow stars to identify themselves as Jews and were not allowed to travel, or even go to their local synagogue, they finally became content just being left alone; that is all they prayed for as Hitler's power swept across Europe. Inside the ghettos they felt a certain security—away from the gestapo (Hitler's officers) and the Hungarian police who ruled the streets outside.

Elie's family lived in a ghetto almost free of guards, so friends managed to sneak in and visit secretly. "Our old servant, Martha, came to see us," Elie wrote. "Weeping bitterly, she begged us to come to her village, where she could give us safe refuge. My father did not want to hear of it. 'You can go if you want to,' he said to me and my older sisters. 'I shall stay here with your mother and the child [Elie's little sister, Tzipora].' Naturally we refused to be separated."

But Hitler couldn't ignore Sighet's 15,000 Jews. To purify Europe he would have to get rid of them. So in the spring of 1944—spring, when fragile wildflowers began to cover the rugged mountainside—Hitler ordered the deportation of all the Jews in Sighet. For their safety, they were told. But they were not told their destination—a Polish town called Oswiecim, better known by its German name, Auschwitz. It was the site of Hitler's largest death camp, where, amid the chaos of World War II, millions of innocent Jews were slaughtered.

Elie Wiesel remembers how people reacted to the deportation orders:

A girl wears the yellow Star of David that all Jews in German-occupied countries were forced to wear.

People were saying: "Who knows? Perhaps we are being deported for our own good. The [battle] front isn't very far off; we shall soon be able to hear the guns. And then the civilian population would be evacuated anyway. . . ." "If you ask me," [someone else said], "the whole business of deportation is just a farce. . . . They just want to steal our jewelry. They know we've buried everything and that they'll have to hunt for it; it's easier when the owners are on holiday. . . ." On holiday! These optimistic speeches, which no one believed, helped to pass the time.

Then the police put the orders into action. "Forward march!" the police yelled. Elie stayed close to his family. "I looked at my little sister, Tzipora," he recalled. "Her fair hair well combed, a red coat over her arm, a little girl of seven. The bundle on her back was too heavy for her. She gritted her teeth. She knew by now it was useless to complain. . . . 'Faster! Faster! Get on with you, lazy swine!' yelled the Hungarian police."

At the railway station "a convoy of cattle wagons

A line of Jewish families awaits deportation at a train station.

was waiting," Elie wrote. "The police made us get in—eighty people in each car. . . . Then the cars were sealed. . . . A prolonged whistle split the air. The wheels began to grind. We were on our way. . . . Two gestapo officers strolled about the platform, smiling."

And Elie Wiesel's childhood came to an end.

Night

Critics have stated that *Night*, Elie Wiesel's book about life and death in concentration camps, is the most powerful, personal account of the Holocaust ever written. Although the work is only 109 pages long, its power is "terrifying," the *New York Times* reported. And Alfred Kazin said, "No one has left behind him so moving a record." One passage from the book has become familiar around the world. It marks the beginning of Elie Wiesel's forever-haunting memory of Auschwitz:

During the Congressional Gold Medal ceremony, Elie Wiesel urges then-president Ronald Reagan to cancel a planned trip to a German cemetery containing the bodies of Nazi storm troopers. Despite Wiesel's entreaties, Reagan went ahead with the visit.

Never shall I forget that night, the first night in camp, which has turned my life into one long night, seven times cursed and seven times sealed. Never shall I forget that smoke. Never shall I forget the little faces of the children, whose bodies I saw turned into wreaths of smoke beneath a silent blue sky.

Never shall I forget those flames which consumed my faith forever. Never shall I forget that nocturnal silence which deprived me, for all eternity, of the desire to live. Never shall I forget those moments which murdered my God and my soul and turned my dreams to dust. Never shall I forget these things, even if I am condemned to live as long as God Himself. Never.

Jews suffered starvation and beatings daily at Auschwitz, but for young, 15-year-old Elie the memory of his father's long, dragged-out death before his own eyes was the most painful torture he endured there. At the same time he never felt as close to his father as he did in the camps. Separated from his mother and sisters, Elie rarely left his father's side.

Everyone knew that in camp the sick and dying would be prime candidates for "selection"—the Nazi's term for choosing those who would be sent to the crematory (furnace) to burn to death. While concerned about his father's health, Elie learned that his mother and little sister, Tzipora, had already been killed. (After the war he discovered that his older sisters had survived.) Elie drew closer and closer to his father.

When winter came, Elie and his father and hundreds of other weak and dying men were transferred to another camp—Buchenwald, in Germany. The train was freezing cold, and they shivered all the way under wet blankets. Elie recalled their arrival:

> It was late at night. The guards came to unload us. The dead were abandoned in the train. Only those who could still stand were able to get out. . . . A hundred of us had got into the wagon. A dozen of us got out—among them, my father and I.

Elie's father became sicker every day at Buchenwald. At night, while lying in his bunk, hot with fever, he would mange a faint call for water, and each time the Nazi officer would yell back, "Quiet!" But his father could barely hear anything around him. Close to death, he kept pleading desperately for water. Finally the Nazi officer struck him on the head with his heavy stick . . . while Elie watched in horror. "I did not move," he wrote later. "I was afraid. . . . I could see he was still breathing. . . . Bending over him I stayed gazing at him for over an hour, engraving into myself the picture of his blood-stained face, his shattered skull."

The next day, January 29, 1945, Elie woke up to find someone else in his father's place. "They must have taken him away before dawn," he wrote, "and carried him to the crematory. He may still have been breathing. . . . I did not weep, and it pained me that I could not weep. But I had no more tears."

After that, nothing mattered to Elie. "Nothing could touch me anymore," he said. All he could think of was "a drop of soup," a bite of bread. Like all the 600 children in Buchenwald, he was starving and could barely walk. Only in his dreams, he told a reporter, did he remain alive. He longed for sleep—when he could return to the past, to his childhood in Sighet, his family, and his grandfather, Dodye Feig, who laughed and sang and told such wonderful stories.

When spring came, Elie didn't notice that the days

A photo taken at the liberation of the Buchenwald concentration camp shows Elie Wiesel. He is in the center bunk and is the furthest to the right.

were getting brighter. Surrounded by death and starvation, he was aware only of night. Nor did he know if Hitler was winning or losing the war against the Allies—the Americans, British, French, and Soviets.

45

But on April 11, 1945, he found out. "At about six o'clock in the evening," he remembered vividly, "the first American tank stood at the gates of Buchenwald." The Nazis surrendered and were taken to American prison camps. The Jews were set free.

How did Elie and the others—who by then were so near death—react to their liberation? They could think only of food. "Not of revenge, not of our families, nothing but bread." American troops took the children to a hospital to help them get well again. Elie suffered from food poisoning and nearly died, but after two weeks in the hospital he began to recover. In his typically simple yet powerful way, he described his emaciated condition:

> One day I was able to get up, after gathering all my strength. I wanted to see myself in the mirror hanging on the opposite wall. I had not seen myself since the ghetto. From the depths of the mirror, a corpse gazed back at me. The look in his eyes, as they stared into mine, has never left me.

A Few Who Cared

Even after the war many people ignored the Jews and other survivors of the Holocaust. To some they were carriers of disease; to others they were a symbol of death. But Wiesel never fails to tell his students and audiences around the world that there were a few who cared. "In remembering the Holocaust," he wrote, "we must not be numbed by the magnitude of its horrors. We must allow ourselves to be moved by the humanity the victims succeeded in preserving at all times. And we must humbly and gratefully look at the few individuals who . . . became our protectors—better yet: our allies and friends."

Those allies and friends included the courageous residents of Le Chambon in south-central France. Adults and children who fled Adolf Hitler's Germany found a safe haven there—even after Hitler's occupation of France. "Jewish children went to school with non-Jewish children," wrote Pierre Sauvage, president of the Friends of Le Chambon. "They played tug-of-war and other games." And, he recalled, "They had a pig named Adolf."

Why the villagers of Le Chambon in particular were

Elie Wiesel stands with other members of the U.S. Holocaust Memorial Council, a group dedicated to making sure that the lessons of the Holocaust are not forgotten.

so courageous and kind is still an unsolved mystery. But Pierre Sauvage gives us a clue: "It is important to know that they were brought up to understand the language of love," he wrote. "When their hearts spoke to them, they first listened, then they acted." In other countries, too, people—ministers, priests, and ordinary citizens—risked their lives to hide Jews during the war.

The Danes also showed special courage to protect them, yet they claimed they were doing only what was natural and human.

But when the Jews tried to leave Europe after the war, they faced new barriers. Even the United States was reluctant to accept Jewish refugees; only the healthiest ones "with voluminous certificates" could obtain visas. "The refugees with the gravest problems, physical or other, who needed help more than their comrades, were welcomed only by Norway," Elie Wiesel wrote.

Orphaned by the Holocaust, young Elie was cared for by the Oeuvres du Secours aux Enfants, a Jewish children's aid society in France. In 1948 he moved to Paris and studied at the Sorbonne. To pay for his education he taught Hebrew and the Bible, directed a choir, and even served as a summer camp counselor. He learned French by reading the works of Jean Racine, and once he mastered the language, he became a journalist. While writing for the Israeli paper *Yedioth Ahronoth,* Wiesel went to India, where he learned English, and wrote a comparative study of

Jewish, Christian, and Hindu beliefs. But he did not write about the Holocaust . . . because it would take years, he said, to find the "right words."

In 1954, following an interview with François Mauriac, the French Catholic writer and Nobel laureate, Wiesel was inspired to break his ten-year silence about his life in the death camps. And in 1958 *La Nuit* (*Night*), originally an 864-page manuscript, was published (in shortened form) in France. He dedicated the book to the memory of his parents and little sister, Tzipora. The first English translation came out in 1960, and after that, Wiesel's writing flourished. He wrote novels, including *Dawn, The Accident, The Town Beyond the Wall, The Gates of the Forest, A Beggar in Jerusalem, The Forgotten,* and many more. He also wrote plays, and in *The Trial of God* he probes the question raised in the Book of Job: What is God's role in human suffering?

The Jews of Silence and *The Testament* deal with anti-Semitism in the former Soviet Union—one of the many countries where he has spoken out on behalf of oppressed Jews and imprisoned dissidents. He has

Marion Wiesel kisses her husband after learning that he has won the Nobel Peace Prize.

gone to South Africa to oppose apartheid, to Central America to help indigenous people in their nonviolent fight for human rights, and to the Middle East to try to end ancient hatreds there. In the early 1990s Wiesel was one of the first to see for himself the bloodshed in Bosnia and to urge foreign help for its victims.

In 1956, after coming to the United States, Wiesel was hit by a taxicab in New York City and confined to a wheelchair for a year. He became a United States citizen in 1963, and six years later began a new life when he married Marion Erster Rose. He had much more in common with her than a love of books and learning. Both were survivors of the Holocaust, and they named their son Shlomo-Elisha, after Wiesel's courageous father, who died in Buchenwald.

It was Marion Wiesel who translated many of her husband's books from French into English, and he has won many literary awards for his work. They include: the Prix Rivarol; the Prix Medicis; the Eleanor Roosevelt Award; the Martin Luther King Medallion; the Prix Livre-Inter; the Prix des Bibliothequares; the Grand Prix de la Littérature de la ville de Paris; and

Elie Wiesel and Egil Aarvik, chairman of the Nobel Peace Prize Committee, arrive for presentation ceremonies in Oslo, Norway.

two National Jewish Book Awards.

In 1986 Elie Wiesel received the world's most distinguished award—the Nobel Peace Prize. In his acceptance speech, delivered in Oslo, Norway, he spoke about the responsibilities involved in seeking peace.

> I remember: it happened yesterday or eternities
> ago. A young Jewish boy discovered the king-
> dom of night. I remember his bewilderment, I
> remember his anguish. It all happened so fast.
> The ghetto. The deportation. The sealed cattle
> car. The fiery altar upon which the history of
> our people and the future of mankind were
> meant to be sacrificed. . . . Sometimes we
> must interfere. When human lives are endan-
> gered, when human dignity is in jeopardy,
> national borders and sensitivities become irrel-
> evant. Wherever men or women are persecuted
> because of their race, religion, or political
> views, that place must—at that moment—
> become the center of the universe.

Today, Elie Wiesel commutes between New York,
where he lives, and Boston University, where he teach-
es. He is Andrew Mellon Professor in the humanities
there, and is a member of the departments of Religion,

Philosophy, and University Professors. (At home he likes to play chess, listen to Bach cantatas—and satisfy his longtime love of chocolate!) As the founding chairman of the United States Holocaust Memorial Council, he shared the podium with President Clinton at the 1993 dedication of the Holocaust Memorial Museum in Washington, D.C. In his speech he remembered those who suffered in the death camps. And he urged the president to do *something* about the continued suffering in Bosnia . . . just as he had asked President Reagan, who awarded him the Congressional Gold Medal, not to visit the military cemetery in Bitburg, Germany, where Nazi officers were buried. "Your place is with the victims," he told the president.

Elie Wiesel is not afraid to speak out on behalf of Holocaust victims, because it is the "human" thing to do, he says. With the resurgence of racism and violence in the world today, he feels it is especially important for young people to work toward a more human world—a world in which compassion for those from cultures other than their own is a major priority.

U.S. Holocaust Memorial Council chairman Harvey M. Meyerhoff, President Bill Clinton, and Elie Wiesel light an eternal flame outside the U.S. Holocaust Memorial Museum.

Toward a More
Humane World

Even without trying, Elie Wiesel has the power to turn nonbelievers into believers, theologian Robert McAfee Brown said. "And [after reading his works] some who did not care have come to care," Brown wrote. But how could anyone not care? Not believe? Though it may seem impossible, there are those who deny that the Holocaust ever happened! Even some highly educated people refuse to believe the facts, and they make up facts of their own to prove their case. Why? Some psychologists believe that certain people can't cope with the awful reality—that evil men like Hitler and his henchmen could exist in the civilized 20th century, let alone conduct such a monstrous massacre. Had Hitler looked like a monster and dressed like one, there would be no doubters. But Hitler wore a uniform and marched around not unlike military officers in any country. And many people in an unsettled country like Germany in the 1930s were looking for leadership and willing to believe in him.

Today, neo-Nazis and white supremacists carry on Hitler's racist philosophy and deny the Holocaust.

Such groups stun compassionate human beings throughout the world. "I'd like to sit them all down," one World War II veteran said, "and show them the pictures I took to document the atrocities at Buchenwald. I'd like to show them where hatred like theirs can lead them . . . but I think they're too dumb to understand."

When asked how he responds to those who deny the Holocaust ever happened, Elie Wiesel answered: "I can only tell you what one survivor feels. More than sadness, he feels dismay, and more than dismay he feels despair, and even more than despair he feels disgust."

"It would be such a blessing," wrote Robert McAfee Brown, "not to have to believe the Holocaust happened. We would be relieved of fears that people are guilty of deep evil; we would be absolved of guilt for possible complicity; we could believe that all is basically well. . . . There is a price paid for such a path, however: attempts to deny a past Holocaust almost ensure that there will be a future one."

To make sure that such a prediction never comes true, Elie Wiesel continues to write and talk about reconciliation and peace:

Elie and Marion Wiesel walk through the gates of the Auschwitz concentration camp with Polish labor leader Lech Walesa in 1988 at the 43rd anniversary of the camp's liberation.

All we want is to create peace and create in peace, and bear witness that man is not necessarily man's enemy, that every war is senseless, that the solution lies in compassion, and that compassion is possible. . . . The very first war, the one between Cain and Abel, taught us that he who kills another kills himself. That is why "Thou shalt not kill" is one of the Ten Commandments.

All those killed in the Holocaust—especially Wiesel's family and friends from Sighet—are never off his mind. And many of them, under different names, come to life in his novels and plays. His grandfather, Dodye Feig, appears often in his writings. Dodye Feig, we remember, was loved for his kindness, and "because of his passion for life, for people, for trees, and books."

And so is Elie Wiesel.

For Further Reading

Brown, Robert McAfee. *Elie Wiesel: Messenger to All Humanity*. Notre Dame: University of Notre Dame Press, 1989.

Frank, Anne. *Anne Frank: The Diary of a Young Girl*. New York: Random House, 1978.

I Dream of Peace: Images of War by Children of Former Yugoslavia. New York: UNICEF/HarperCollins, 1994.

Keneally, Thomas. *Schindler's List*. New York: Simon & Schuster, 1993.

Rittner, Carol and Sondra Myers, eds. *The Courage to Care*. New York: New York University Press, 1989.

Volovkova, Hana, ed. *I Never Saw Another Butterfly: Children's Drawings and Poems from Terezin Concentration Camp, 1942-1944*. New York: Pantheon, 1993.

Wiesel, Elie. *Legends of Our Time*. New York: Holt, Rinehart and Winston, 1968.

_____. *Night*. New York: Bantam Books, 1989.

Steven Spielberg's *Schindler's List,* based on Thomas Keneally's book, is an excellent film that portrays the life of a man who helped rescue many Jews from the Holocaust.

Index

About the Author

Caroline Evensen Lazo was born in Minneapolis, Minnesota. She spent much of her childhood visiting museums and attending plays written by her mother, Isobel Evensen, whose work earned national acclaim and became a lasting source of inspiration for her daughter.

Ms. Lazo attended the University of Oslo, Norway, and received a B.A. in art history from the University of Minnesota. She has written extensively about art and architecture and is the author of many books for young people, including *The Terra Cotta Army of Emperor Qin*, *Missing Treasure*, and *Endangered Species*.